This mandala coloring book belongs to:

____

TIPS FOR USING THIS COLORING BOOK:

1. Take this priceless opportunity to sit next to your grandchild, as you discuss the fun facts and color together.

2. Large print images with minimal to medium detail are similar for grandma and grandchild, so they're easy to color for both grandma and grandchild.

3. Extra almost blank pages (with tiny cute hedgehog doodles in the corners) have been added to prevent bleeding or remove the pages to color.

4. Place a sheet of paper behind the pages to allow the optional use of markers, gel pens, crayons, or colored pencils, if pressing hard.

5. Discuss the shape of the mandalas; the circle has the same shape of a plate, coin, and wheel. Discuss other things that are circles.

6. Explain symmetry and the shape of the mandala (circle):
diameter-distance across, radius-distance from the diameter to the edge, and it's a shape without corners.

7. Discuss and name the seasons as you color these mandalas.

8. Allow your child to express his/her feelings as they color, even if it means coloring outside the lines.

9. Play inspirational music as you color to create a relaxing atmosphere.

10. Use for coloring (or art therapy) at all ages for mindfulness, relaxation, reflection, self-knowledge, and wisdom.

By Florabella Publishing

By Florabella Publishing

Mandalas are the most ancient form of art.

A mandala is usually the shape of a circle.

Babies prefer to look at a circle rather than other shapes.

After scribbling, the first shape a toddler
draws is a circle.

Name other things around you that are in the shape of a circle?

Adults draw circles to reconnect with their childhood.

Looking through a kaleidoscope is one way to experience mandala art.

Some artists use a dinner plate as a form for designing a mandala.

Artists may use old compact discs or records to form their mandalas.

A mandala reflects the things in our life;
family, friends, and community.

Many mandalas have symmetrical images.

Do you see symmetry in either of these mandalas?

Artists sometimes use sand, clay, or canvas to create a mandala design.

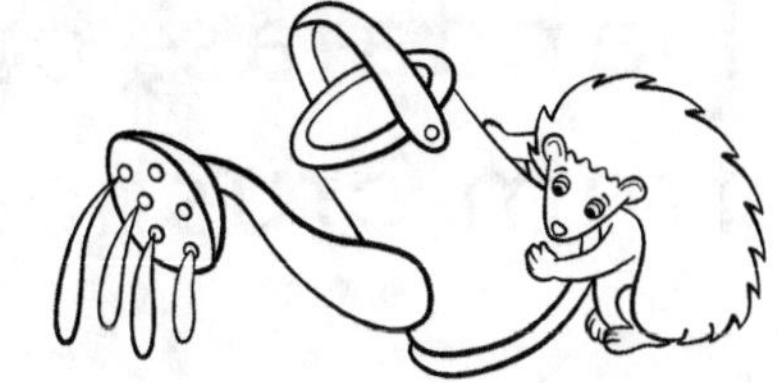

Mandalas, created with colored sand are from crushed semi-precious stones.

A group mandala is a fun way for children to celebrate a birthday or holiday.

The circular mandala reflects many things found in nature such as the earth, sun, and moon.

Mandalas are found in all cultures throughout the world!

florabellapublishing.com
florabellapublishing@yahoo.com